Using NLP to Boost Creative Thinking and Problem-Solving Skills

By Rex Morton

Copyright Page

information the organization or website may provide or recommendations it might make. Furthermore, the author does not guarantee the accuracy of the information these resources provide.

The use of any information provided in this book is solely at your own risk.

Welcome to an exciting journey of discovery and transformation! The fact that you're reading this tells me you're ready to unlock new doors in your mind, unleash your creative potential, and elevate your problem-solving skills to a whole new level. This journey, at its core, is about enhancing your creativity and problem-solving skills using an approach known as Neuro-Linguistic Programming, or NLP.

Neuro-Linguistic Programming is a fascinating field that combines insights from psychology, linguistics, and neuroscience to better understand and influence human thought and behavior. NLP, which was created in the 1970s by Richard Bandler and John Grinder, examines the connections between our cognitive processes (neuro), our linguistic interactions, and our behavioral and emotional conditioning. This approach's principles have been successfully applied in a variety of fields, including communication, business, and personal development.

But what does this have to do with creativity and problem-solving? More than you might think. Our brains are not static entities but dynamic systems capable of learning, adapting, and creating. NLP techniques allow us to tap into this potential, challenge our conventional ways of thinking, and stimulate our creative abilities.

Let me share a personal story. I once met a brilliant scientist named Laura, who had hit a seemingly insurmountable wall with her research. She felt stuck and frustrated, unable to generate fresh ideas or find innovative solutions. When she encountered NLP, she was skeptical but desperate for a breakthrough. She began applying NLP techniques to her situation, and the results were astonishing. Not only did she overcome her research obstacles, but she also unlocked a wellspring of creativity she didn't know she possessed. Her colleagues noticed the change, and she started to get invited to participate in more projects. NLP transformed not only her professional life but also her personal life.

In the chapters that follow, we will delve into the principles of NLP, its fundamental techniques, and its applications to enhance creativity and problem-solving skills. We will learn about the structure of the human mind, how we communicate, and how our thoughts shape our behaviors. We will also explore a wealth of NLP techniques designed to stimulate creative thinking and facilitate effective problem-solving.

As we progress through the book, we will guide you through practical exercises, providing real-life case studies, and tackling common challenges you might face along the way. By the end, we hope to have provided you with a solid foundation in NLP, and more importantly, practical skills that you can apply immediately in your daily life to boost your creativity and problem-solving capabilities.

Whether you're an artist seeking inspiration, a professional facing complex challenges, or simply someone who wants to get more out of life, we believe that NLP holds a key to unlock your potential. Embarking on this journey may be one of the most rewarding experiences of your life. Let's begin.

In this chapter, we will delve into the foundational elements of Neuro-Linguistic Programming (NLP), tracing its history and development, examining its key principles and presuppositions, and familiarizing ourselves with some common terminology.

History and Development of NLP

The genesis of NLP goes back to the early 1970s. It was then that Richard Bandler, a psychology student, and John Grinder, an assistant professor of linguistics, began a fruitful collaboration at the University of California, Santa Cruz. They aimed to uncover why some individuals were extraordinarily successful in their respective fields while others with similar backgrounds and skills struggled.

In their pursuit of answers, Bandler and Grinder studied the works and methods of renowned therapists such as Fritz Perls, Virginia Satir, and Milton Erickson. By modeling these exceptionally effective individuals, they formulated a set of tools and techniques that would eventually become known as Neuro-Linguistic Programming. The name itself reflects the interconnectedness of our neurology (Neuro), our language (Linguistic), and our learned behaviors (Programming).

Key Principles and Presuppositions of NLP

There are several key principles and presuppositions in NLP that serve as its backbone. Here are a few of the most significant ones:

The Map is Not the Territory: This principle asserts that our perception of reality is not reality itself but our 'map' or mental model of it. We respond to our maps, not to reality.

There is No Failure, Only Feedback: In NLP, there is no such thing as failure, only learning experiences. If one approach doesn't work, it's an opportunity to try something different and adjust our strategies.

The Meaning of Communication is the Response You Get: This emphasizes the importance of flexibility in communication. If your communication doesn't get the desired response, it's up to you to alter your communication.

The Mind and Body are Parts of the Same System: Our thoughts, feelings, and physiology are interconnected. Changes in one can lead to changes in the others.

If One Person Can Do Something, Anyone Can Learn to Do It: This is the principle of 'modeling'. If someone has a skill or ability, it can be modeled and taught to others.

Common Terminology Used in NLP

As we delve deeper into NLP, we will encounter a range of specific terms. Here are a few essential ones to get started:

Anchoring: The process of associating an internal response with an external or internal stimulus, allowing the response to be recalled or accessed at will.

Rapport: A state of understanding and mutual responsiveness between two or more people.

Reframing: The process of changing the way one perceives an experience, thus changing its meaning and impact.

Submodalities: The specific properties or characteristics of our internal representations, including sight, sound, feeling, taste, and smell.

Modeling: The process of replicating the behavior, skill, or ability of others.

By understanding the origins, principles, and language of NLP, we set a solid foundation for the practical application of NLP techniques. In the next chapter, we will delve into the mysteries of the human mind and explore how NLP interacts with our neural, linguistic, and programming systems.

To understand how Neuro-Linguistic Programming (NLP) might improve our creativity and problem-solving abilities, it is important to first comprehend the brain, the organ where all of this magic takes place. All of our thoughts, feelings, and actions are controlled by this intricate network of synapses and neurons.

How the Brain Works

Our brains are made up of roughly 86 billion neurons, interconnected via trillions of synapses, forming a highly complex network. These neurons communicate with each other using electrical and chemical signals. This dynamic interaction shapes our thoughts, emotions, and behaviors.

The brain is composed of different regions, each with specialized functions. For example, the frontal lobes are involved in decision-making and problem-solving, while the limbic system plays a crucial role in our emotional responses.

Patterns of thought, emotions, and behavior are formed as our brain creates neural pathways, often called 'habits of mind'. When we repeatedly think in a certain way or perform a specific behavior, these neural pathways are strengthened, making it easier to repeat these thought patterns or behaviors in the future. This is sometimes referred to as 'neurons that fire together, wire together'.

Conscious and Unconscious Mind

Our mind can be divided into two main components: the conscious and the unconscious.

The conscious mind, often likened to the tip of an iceberg visible above the water, includes everything we're currently aware of. It's our active thinking part, the 'here and now' of our mental life.

The unconscious mind, like the vast hidden part of the iceberg beneath the surface, includes everything that we're not currently aware of. It's a reservoir of feelings, thoughts, urges, memories, and automatic skills (like driving a car) that are outside our conscious awareness. Despite its hidden nature, our unconscious mind greatly influences our behaviors, decisions, and reactions.

NLP's Interaction with Neural, Linguistic, and Programming Systems

Neuro-Linguistic Programming, true to its name, operates at the intersection of these aspects of our mind and brain.

Neuro: NLP recognizes that all our behaviors stem from neurological processes. It uses techniques designed to influence these processes and, consequently, change our behaviors and responses.

Linguistic: NLP understands that our language affects how we interact with the world and how we represent it in our minds. By examining and modifying our language and communication, we can change our perceptions and responses.

Programming: NLP sees our patterns of thought and behavior as learned programs that can be altered. By identifying and modifying these programs using a variety of techniques, we can change how we react, perceive, and make decisions.

Understanding the workings of the human mind forms the basis for applying NLP techniques. By grasping the brain's function and the interplay between conscious and unconscious processes, we can better appreciate how NLP can help us boost our creative thinking and problem-solving abilities. In the next chapter, we will explore how we process information and how language shapes our reality.

Chapter 4: The NLP Communication Model

The Neuro-Linguistic Programming (NLP) Communication Model provides a framework for understanding how we perceive, process, and respond to the world around us. It delves into the role of our senses, the power of language, and the possibility of altering our thought patterns and behaviors, or "programming."

Processing Information Using Our Five Senses

The first step in the NLP Communication Model is to understand how we gather information from the world around us. This process is primarily accomplished through our five senses: sight (visual), hearing (auditory), touch (kinesthetic), smell (olfactory), and taste (gustatory). We perceive our reality through these senses, forming our individual understanding of the world. This sensory input is then filtered through our personal experiences, beliefs, values, and cultural background, among other things. As a result, the world we perceive is a subjective interpretation, not an objective reality.

The Role of Language in Shaping Our Reality

The next component in the NLP Communication Model is the role of language. Language, an integral part of our communication, plays a significant role in shaping our perception of reality. Through language, we assign meaning to our sensory experiences, transforming raw data into understandable information.

The words we use and the way we use them - our syntax, metaphors, and speech patterns - create a linguistic map of our world. NLP studies these linguistic patterns, recognizing that by altering our language, we can change our perception and experience of the world.

Programming to Change Thought Patterns and Behaviors

The final component of the NLP Communication Model is programming. Programming, in this context, refers to the notion that our thoughts, emotions, and behaviors are interconnected and can be changed.

Once we become aware of our patterns of thought and behavior, we can 'reprogram' them if they're unhelpful or limiting. Using specific NLP techniques, such as reframing or anchoring, we can alter these patterns to serve us better. For example, we can change negative thought patterns into positive ones or modify unproductive behaviors into productive ones.

In essence, the NLP Communication Model illustrates that our understanding of the world is a product of our sensory perceptions, filtered and interpreted through our personal and linguistic lenses. Recognizing this allows us to 'update our programming' - changing our thought patterns and behaviors to improve our experiences and interactions with the world around us.

In the next chapters, we will delve into how we can use NLP to enhance our creative thinking and problem-solving skills, applying this understanding of perception, language, and programming to reach our full potential.

As we delve deeper into our journey of personal and professional growth through Neuro-Linguistic Programming (NLP), it becomes vital to understand and appreciate the role of creativity in this process. In this chapter, we will explore the essence of creativity, its importance in problem-solving, and how NLP techniques can be employed to boost our creative thinking.

Defining Creativity

Creativity is often associated with artists, musicians, and writers. However, it is a universal human capability that extends far beyond the arts. Essentially, creativity is the capacity to generate novel and valuable ideas or solutions. It entails thinking creatively, connecting ideas that at first glance appear unrelated, and adopting a fresh viewpoint.

In the context of NLP, creativity isn't just a trait possessed by a select few but a skill that can be nurtured and enhanced in anyone willing to explore and experiment with their thinking patterns.

The Importance of Creativity in Problem-Solving

Creative thinking is at the heart of effective problem-solving. When faced with challenges, our first instinct often is to rely on familiar strategies or solutions. While these can be helpful in some situations, they may prove insufficient or ineffective when dealing with new, complex, or ambiguous problems.

This is where creativity comes into play. It allows us to generate a wide range of potential solutions, explore different perspectives, and innovate new approaches that wouldn't be apparent through conventional thinking. The ability to think creatively makes us more adaptable and capable of tackling diverse challenges.

Enhancing Creativity with NLP

NLP offers a wealth of techniques to stimulate and enhance our creativity. These methods work by breaking down limiting beliefs, expanding our perceptual filters, and encouraging the generation of new, diverse ideas.

For instance, techniques like reframing help us to look at situations from different perspectives, enabling us to come up with unique solutions. The Visual-Kinesthetic Dissociation technique, also known as the 'Swish', can help us overcome mental blocks that impede our creative thinking.

Other techniques, like the Disney Strategy, designed after the creative process of Walt Disney, can guide us in nurturing our dreams (Dreamer stage), turning them into actionable plans (Realist stage), and refining those plans (Critic stage).

By learning and applying these NLP techniques, we can develop our creative thinking skills, enriching not only our problem-solving abilities but also our personal and professional lives.

As we continue our journey, the following chapters will guide you through these specific NLP techniques, explaining how they work and how you can apply them to boost your creativity and problem-solving skills.

Boosting creative thinking with Neuro-Linguistic Programming (NLP) involves an array of methods and practices. This chapter will guide you through various NLP techniques designed to enhance creativity, provide practical exercises to stimulate creative thinking, and present real-life case studies to demonstrate the effectiveness of these techniques.

NLP Techniques Designed to Enhance Creativity

1. The Disney Strategy: This technique, inspired by Walt Disney's creative process, involves three distinct stages - the Dreamer, the Realist, and the Critic. Each stage helps us nurture ideas, translate them into actionable plans, and then evaluate them for potential pitfalls. For instance, while brainstorming for a new business venture, you might first let your imagination run wild without constraints (Dreamer), then start figuring out logistics and operations (Realist), and finally, evaluate the plan for possible issues and improvements (Critic).

2. Reframing: Reframing is a powerful NLP technique used to change the way we perceive events or experiences, thereby changing their impact. By consciously choosing to view a problem or situation from a new angle, we can generate creative solutions that might not have been apparent otherwise. For instance, viewing a failure not as a setback but as a learning opportunity allows for creative growth and development.

3. Belief Change: Often, our beliefs can limit our creative thinking. NLP offers techniques to challenge and change these limiting beliefs, freeing us up to think more creatively. For instance, if you believe you're not a 'creative person', this belief may hinder your creative thinking. NLP techniques can help you challenge this belief and replace it with a more empowering one, such as 'I can enhance my creativity with practice and openness'.

Practical Exercises to Stimulate Creative Thinking

1. Random Word Generation: Write down a problem you're trying to solve. Then generate a random word (using a random word generator or just picking a word from a book). Try to connect this random word to your problem and see if it sparks any new ideas or solutions.

2. The Six Thinking Hats: Based on Edward de Bono's methodology, this exercise involves viewing a problem from six different perspectives (Information, Emotions, Critical judgment, Optimistic response, Creativity, and Process). By consciously switching 'hats', you can explore a broader range of solutions.

Hypothetical Case Studies

1. Hypothetical Case Study – Reframing in Advertising: An advertising firm was struggling with a campaign for a brand of shoes that were durable but not very fashionable. By reframing the problem, they decided to market the shoes as 'anti-fashion' and celebrated their durability and practicality. The campaign was a huge success, demonstrating the power of reframing to stimulate creative solutions.

2. Hypothetical Case Study – Belief Change in Personal Development: A woman felt stuck in her career, believing she wasn't 'creative enough' for better opportunities. Through NLP belief change techniques, she replaced her limiting belief with 'I am continually developing my creative thinking skills.' With her new belief, she started exploring creative solutions at work and soon received a promotion.

Through these NLP techniques, practical exercises, and real-life case studies, we see how we can effectively enhance our creative thinking. By using these tools and practicing regularly, we can boost our ability to generate innovative ideas and solve problems creatively.

Chapter 7: The Power of Problem-Solving

Effective problem-solving is a crucial skill for both personal and professional success. This chapter explores the importance of honing these skills, the stages of problem-solving, and how creative thinking contributes significantly to this process.

The Importance of Effective Problem-Solving Skills

Problem-solving is an integral part of life. From minor day-to-day decisions to major business strategies, our ability to solve problems effectively greatly influences our outcomes.

In our personal life, effective problem-solving skills help us navigate relationships, make informed decisions, and overcome hurdles. Professionally, these skills become even more critical. Businesses thrive on their ability to identify and solve problems efficiently, be it related to their products, services, or internal processes. Leaders and employees who can successfully solve problems are considered invaluable assets to their organizations.

Moreover, in today's fast-paced, ever-changing world, the ability to solve complex and unfamiliar problems is highly sought after. It provides us with adaptability and resilience, making us better prepared to face and overcome challenges.

The Stages of Problem-Solving

Problem-solving typically involves several stages:

Identifying the Problem: This involves recognizing that a problem exists and clearly defining it. It's crucial to understand the problem thoroughly, including its context and impact.

Analyzing the Problem: This stage involves gathering as much information about the problem as possible, including its causes, effects, and related factors.

Generating Solutions: This is where you brainstorm possible solutions. This stage greatly benefits from creative thinking, as the more diverse the solutions considered, the better the final decision is likely to be.

Evaluating and Selecting Solutions: In this stage, you assess each potential solution based on its feasibility, potential impact, resources required, and other relevant factors. Then, you select the best solution.

Implementing the Solution: This involves carrying out the chosen solution and monitoring its effectiveness in solving the problem.

Reviewing the Results: After implementing the solution, it's important to review its effectiveness and make necessary adjustments. This stage provides valuable learning for future problem-solving.

Creative Thinking in Effective Problem-Solving

Creative thinking plays a pivotal role in the problem-solving process, particularly during the generation of solutions. The ability to think 'outside the box' allows us to come up with a wide range of potential solutions, including novel and unconventional ones.

Creativity is also valuable in the problem-identification stage, where it can help us notice problems that others might overlook. Furthermore, in the evaluation stage, creative thinking can help us envision the potential impacts of different solutions, aiding in the decision-making process.

The use of Neuro-Linguistic Programming (NLP) can significantly enhance our creative thinking, and thus our problem-solving capabilities. In the next chapter, we will delve into specific NLP techniques designed to improve our problem-solving skills, providing practical examples and exercises.

Building on the fundamentals of Neuro-Linguistic Programming (NLP) and understanding the role of creativity, we now look at specific NLP techniques that can enhance our problem-solving skills. This chapter will provide an in-depth look into these techniques, guide you through their implementation, and present case studies showcasing these methods in action.

NLP Techniques for Improving Problem-Solving Skills

1. Perceptual Positions: This technique involves viewing a problem from different perspectives (first, second, and third positions). The first position is your perspective, the second is the other person's perspective, and the third is an independent observer's perspective. This technique can help generate fresh insights and diverse solutions.

2. The Meta-Model: The Meta-Model is a set of questions designed to uncover the underlying structure of your thoughts or someone else's. By challenging distortions, deletions, and generalizations in our thinking, the Meta-Model helps us clarify problems and opens up new possibilities for solutions.

3. The Six-Step Reframing Technique: This technique helps identify and modify unwanted behaviors or reactions that might be hindering our problem-solving abilities. It involves identifying the behavior, communicating with the part of you responsible for it, exploring its positive intent, brainstorming new behaviors, integrating the new behavior, and testing it.

Step-by-Step Guides to Implementing These Techniques

Perceptual Positions Exercise:

Think of a problem and view it from your perspective. Notice what you see, hear, and feel.

Now imagine stepping into the shoes of another person involved in the problem. Observe the situation from their viewpoint. What new insights do you gain?

Next, imagine viewing the problem from a detached, third-party perspective. What do you notice from this viewpoint?

The Meta-Model Exercise:

Write down a problem or challenge you're facing.

Begin asking Meta-Model questions, such as "What specifically makes this a problem? How does this prevent me from achieving my goal? Who says it has to be this way?"

The Six-Step Reframing Exercise:

Identify an unwanted behavior or response related to a problem.

Have a mental conversation with the part of you responsible for this behavior, asking it to reveal its positive intention.

Brainstorm new behaviors that could achieve the same positive intention but in a more beneficial way.

Ask the part if it's willing to try these new behaviors.

Imagine yourself in a situation where you typically exhibit the unwanted behavior, but this time, apply the new behavior.

Test this new behavior in real life and observe the outcomes.

Hypothetical Case Studies Demonstrating These Techniques in Action

Hypothetical Case Study – Perceptual Positions in Mediation: A business mediator used the perceptual positions technique to resolve a conflict between two partners. By encouraging them to view the problem from each other's perspectives and from an outsider's viewpoint, they gained new insights, leading to a mutual agreement and resolution of the conflict.

Hypothetical Case Study – The Meta-Model in Coaching: A life coach used the Meta-Model to help a client who felt stuck in her career. By asking Meta-Model questions, the coach helped the client clarify her actual problem (lack of self-confidence, not lack of opportunities as she initially thought), leading to targeted solutions.

Hypothetical Case Study – The Six-Step Reframing in Personal Development: A man who procrastinated frequently used the six-step reframing technique. He discovered that his procrastination was a way of avoiding potential failure (the positive intent). He found alternative behaviors, such as breaking tasks into smaller parts and setting realistic goals, which still avoided potential failure but without the procrastination. He reported significant improvements in his productivity.

Through these NLP techniques and their practical implementation, we can significantly enhance our problem-solving skills. The next chapter will delve into how you can practice and master these techniques for ongoing personal and professional development.

This chapter synthesizes all the elements discussed so far—Neuro-Linguistic Programming (NLP), creative thinking, and problem-solving—into a cohesive and practical approach. We will outline strategies for continued practice and development of these skills and share inspiring stories from people who have successfully applied these techniques in their lives.

Combining the Elements of NLP, Creative Thinking, and Problem-Solving

To combine these elements effectively, it's helpful to understand them as a three-part process that continuously interacts and influences one another.

NLP as the Foundation: NLP serves as the base, providing techniques to better understand and modify our thought patterns, behaviors, and communication. It's the toolset we use to enhance our mental capacities.

Creative Thinking as the Catalyst: Once we've harnessed the power of NLP, we can apply these techniques to boost our creative thinking. Creativity allows us to generate diverse and innovative solutions to problems, making it the catalyst in this process.

Problem-Solving as the Application: Finally, we apply our enhanced creativity to the process of problem-solving. This is where we see the tangible benefits of our enhanced abilities, as we're able to solve problems more effectively and innovatively.

A practical example could be a team leader dealing with conflict within the team. They could use NLP techniques like the Meta-Model to understand the core of the conflict (NLP as the foundation), use creative thinking exercises like the Six Thinking Hats to generate diverse solutions (creative thinking as the catalyst), and finally apply these solutions in a structured problem-solving process (problem-solving as the application).

Strategies for Ongoing Practice and Development of These Skills

Consistent Practice: Like any skill, consistency is key in developing NLP techniques, creativity, and problem-solving abilities. Set aside some time each day to practice these techniques, even if it's just for a few minutes.

Real-life Application: Try to apply these techniques to real-life situations. Start with small, everyday problems before progressing to bigger, more complex ones.

Continual Learning: Stay open to learning more about NLP and other related fields. Attend workshops, read books, or enroll in online courses.

Finding a Mentor or Coach: A mentor or coach who is proficient in NLP can provide personalized guidance, feedback, and support as you develop these skills.

Hypothetical Stories and Experiences from People Who Have Successfully Applied These Techniques

Story 1 - A Business Leader: A CEO of a small tech startup was facing a creative block when developing a new product. After learning about NLP, she started using techniques like reframing and belief change to overcome limiting beliefs around creativity. She also began utilizing creative thinking exercises in team meetings. With these methods, not only did she overcome her creative block, but her team also came up with an innovative product idea that significantly boosted the company's success.

Story 2 - A Teacher: A high school teacher was struggling with classroom management. He decided to use NLP techniques to understand the problem from different perspectives. He applied the perceptual positions technique, which helped him understand his students better and generate creative solutions for classroom management. He found that his relationship with his students improved dramatically, and the classroom environment became more conducive to learning.

These stories demonstrate the power of combining NLP, creative thinking, and problem-solving. In the final chapter, we will provide additional resources and paths for further exploration to continue your journey in mastering these skills.

Despite the effectiveness of Neuro-Linguistic Programming (NLP) in enhancing creative thinking and problem-solving skills, individuals might encounter certain challenges and obstacles along the way. This chapter aims to identify these common hurdles and offer strategies to overcome them, using NLP techniques. Furthermore, we'll discuss ways to maintain motivation and consistency in practicing these skills.

Recognizing Common Obstacles that Hinder Creative Thinking and Problem-Solving

Limiting Beliefs: One of the most common obstacles is the presence of limiting beliefs about one's abilities to think creatively or solve problems effectively. Phrases like "I'm not a creative person" or "I'm not good at problem-solving" are indicators of such beliefs.

Fear of Failure: Fear of making mistakes or failing can inhibit both creative thinking and problem-solving. This fear often leads to risk-aversion and hinders out-of-the-box thinking.

Stress and Overwhelm: High stress levels can interfere with clear thinking and creativity. Moreover, facing a complex problem can sometimes feel overwhelming, making the problem-solving process daunting.

Strategies for Overcoming These Obstacles Using NLP Techniques

NLP Techniques to Overcome Limiting Beliefs:

One powerful NLP technique to address limiting beliefs is reframing. For instance, if you hold the belief, "I'm not a creative person," you could reframe it as, "I haven't developed my creativity yet." This shifts the belief from a fixed state to something that can be improved upon, enabling a growth mindset.

NLP Techniques to Address Fear of Failure:

The Swish Technique can be beneficial here. Visualize a scenario where you're afraid of failing, and then create a more positive image where you're succeeding or dealing with failure constructively. "Swish" the negative image with the positive one repeatedly until the positive image becomes your automatic response to the thought of failure.

NLP Techniques to Reduce Stress and Overwhelm:

Anchoring is an NLP technique that can help manage stress levels. Find a physical gesture (an anchor), such as tapping your fingers together, that you can associate with a calm and relaxed state. Once this association is strong, you can use the anchor whenever you feel stressed or overwhelmed to bring back the calm state.

Ways to Maintain Motivation and Consistency in Practicing These Skills

Set Clear Goals: Having clear goals related to enhancing your creative thinking and problem-solving skills can provide direction and motivation.

Track Your Progress: Regularly tracking your progress can be a strong motivator. Keep a journal of the NLP techniques you're practicing, the problems you're tackling, and the creative solutions you're coming up with.

Celebrate Small Wins: Don't wait until a big problem is solved to celebrate. Acknowledge and celebrate small victories and improvements along the way to keep your morale high.

Find a Community or Accountability Partner: Having someone else to share your progress, challenges, and victories with can significantly increase your motivation and consistency. Consider joining an NLP or personal development group, or find a friend or colleague who's also interested in these skills.

Overcoming these challenges and maintaining motivation in your practice are significant aspects of your journey with NLP, creative thinking, and problem-solving. Remember, the goal isn't perfection but continual growth and development. In the next chapter, we'll provide further resources for continued learning and exploration in these fields.

Incorporating Neuro-Linguistic Programming (NLP) techniques into our daily lives doesn't have to be an intimidating task. In this chapter, we'll discuss practical tips for using NLP techniques in everyday activities, how to build a lifestyle that encourages creativity and effective problem-solving, and the importance of lifelong learning and development.

Practical Tips for Incorporating NLP Techniques into Everyday Activities

NLP in Communication:

Active listening is a crucial part of effective communication. By consciously practicing NLP techniques such as mirroring (reflecting another person's body language) and paraphrasing (repeating the speaker's message in your own words), you can improve understanding and empathy in your daily conversations.

For example, during a family dinner, you could practice mirroring your partner's gestures and posture subtly. This can lead to a deeper sense of connection and rapport.

NLP for Personal Growth:

Self-reflection is a vital part of personal growth. The NLP Meta-Model — a set of specific questions designed to clarify information and challenge limitations — can be used in personal journaling or self-talk to challenge limiting beliefs and explore personal potential.

For instance, if you find yourself thinking, "I can't do this task," you could use the Meta-Model to ask yourself, "What specifically can't I do?" or "Have I ever done a similar task successfully?"

Building a Lifestyle that Encourages Creativity and Effective Problem-Solving

Developing a Growth Mindset:

Cultivating a growth mindset — the belief that abilities and intelligence can be developed through hard work, good strategies, and input from others — can greatly foster creativity and effective problem-solving. You can practice this by embracing challenges, persisting in the face of setbacks, and viewing effort as the path to mastery.

Creating an Enriching Environment:

The environment around us can significantly impact our creative thinking and problem-solving abilities. Surrounding yourself with diverse influences, such as books, art, different cultures, and perspectives, can stimulate creative thinking. Having a quiet space for reflection can also aid in effective problem-solving.

For example, you could dedicate a corner of your home to creativity, filled with art supplies, inspiring books, and images. This can become your go-to spot whenever you need to think creatively or solve a problem.

Encouragement for Lifelong Learning and Development of These Skills

Continuous Practice: NLP, like any other skill, requires continuous practice. Remember, progress is better than perfection. Celebrate each step forward in your journey.

Keep Exploring: The field of NLP is vast and continuously evolving. Stay updated with the latest research and techniques. Attend workshops, seminars, or take online courses.

Stay Curious: Maintain a sense of curiosity and wonder. It's a fuel for creativity and problem-solving. Whether it's asking more questions or exploring new hobbies, nurture your curiosity.

Incorporating NLP techniques into your daily life and nurturing a lifestyle that encourages creativity and problem-solving can be transformative. Remember, this is a journey of self-growth and discovery. In the final chapter, we will wrap up our journey and guide you towards further resources for continued learning in these fields.

As we arrive at the end of our journey, it's time to summarize our key learnings and envision the impact of Neuro-Linguistic Programming (NLP) on our future. NLP, when combined with creative thinking and problem-solving skills, has the potential to bring transformative changes not only in our personal lives but also in broader societal contexts.

Summarizing the Book's Main Points and Takeaways

NLP Basics: NLP is a potent strategy that aids in comprehending and modifying our mental processes, behaviors, and communication. Its foundation is the notion that our brains, language, and actions are interrelated and that they may be trained to produce specific results.

Understanding the Human Mind: The human mind, with its conscious and unconscious elements, is a key player in how we perceive and interact with the world. NLP provides tools to interact effectively with our minds.

Creativity and Problem-Solving: NLP can be used to enhance creativity and improve problem-solving skills. Creative thinking helps generate diverse solutions, while effective problem-solving applies these solutions in a structured manner.

Overcoming Challenges: Like any journey, mastering NLP and improving creativity and problem-solving will have its challenges. Techniques like reframing, the Swish technique, and anchoring can help overcome common obstacles like limiting beliefs, fear of failure, and stress.

Daily Application: NLP techniques can be incorporated into our everyday lives, making them a part of our communication, personal growth, and lifestyle.

Envisioning the Future of NLP and Its Impact on Creative Thinking and Problem-Solving

As our understanding of the human mind deepens, the potential applications and impact of NLP are likely to expand. In the future, we may see NLP techniques becoming more mainstream, potentially being integrated into educational curricula to help children develop effective communication, creative thinking, and problem-solving skills early on.

In the professional world, these skills are increasingly valued. As we continue to automate routine tasks, the human capacity for creative thought and innovative problem-solving becomes our unique advantage. Thus, NLP could play a critical role in professional development and success in various fields.

Final Words of Inspiration and Motivation to Continue the NLP Journey

The journey you've embarked on by reading this book is a powerful one. You've taken the first steps towards enhancing your creative thinking and problem-solving skills using NLP. The road may be challenging at times, but the rewards are worth it.

Remember, the application of NLP isn't just about the techniques—it's a mindset. It's about recognizing your potential to shape your reality, grow beyond perceived limitations, and continuously learn and adapt.

Don't be disheartened if progress seems slow or if old patterns creep back in. Be patient with yourself, celebrate every victory—no matter how small—and keep going.

Your journey with NLP doesn't end with this book—it's just the beginning. Continue exploring, practicing, and applying what you've learned. The power to change your life is in your hands.

Thank you for joining us on this journey. We hope that you're as excited as we are about the possibilities that NLP brings to our lives. Remember: The future isn't something that happens to us—it's something we create. Let's create a future full of creativity, effective problem-solving, and personal growth. Good luck on your continued journey with NLP!

About the Author

Rex Morton is a renowned author and researcher in the United Kingdom with a passionate interest in the human mind, specifically in Cognitive Behavioural Therapy (CBT) and Neuro-Linguistic Programming (NLP).

Morton has spent a considerable portion of his professional life diving deep into the theories and principles that form the backbone of these two compelling fields. His fascination with NLP led him to complete an extensive certification program, solidifying his understanding of this innovative approach to understanding human behaviour.

Although Morton does not have clinical experience, his intense curiosity and dedication to studying these subjects have made him a respected figure in the field. He has thoroughly researched the integration of NLP techniques into CBT, offering fresh perspectives and insights into how these two methodologies can complement each other to enhance understanding of human cognition and behaviour.

As an author, Morton has successfully communicated his knowledge and passion to a broader audience, making complex psychological theories accessible to professionals and interested laypersons. His writing is characterized by a clear, engaging style and a focus on the practical application of theories, making them relevant to everyday life.

In his personal life, Morton is an ardent lover of the natural world, often spending his free time exploring the British countryside. His passion for landscape photography allows him to capture and share the beauty of these excursions. Despite his accomplishments, Morton is known for his humility and eagerness to continue learning. His work continues to inspire those interested in the intricate workings of the human mind and the exciting possibilities presented by the integration of NLP and CBT.

If you've found the content of this book enlightening and wish to continue your journey of understanding the human mind, I warmly invite you to visit my website at www.rexmorton.com. The website serves as a hub of knowledge where I share my latest findings, thoughts, and insights on the integration of NLP and CBT.

I also encourage you to subscribe to the newsletter available on the website. By subscribing, you'll receive regular updates on a range of topics, from detailed discussions on specific NLP techniques and their application in CBT, to the latest research in the field.

The newsletter is also the first place I'll share news of upcoming releases. Whether it's the announcement of a new book, the launch of an online course, newsletter subscribers will be the first to know. This is a great opportunity to continue learning directly from me, deepening your understanding of NLP and CBT, and enhancing your skills in applying these techniques in your own life or professional practice.

I'm looking forward to sharing this journey with you.